Date Due

BRODART   Cat. No. 23 233   Printed in U.S.A.

$2000 7/01 Follett

STONES AND BONES!

How Archaeologists Trace Human Origins

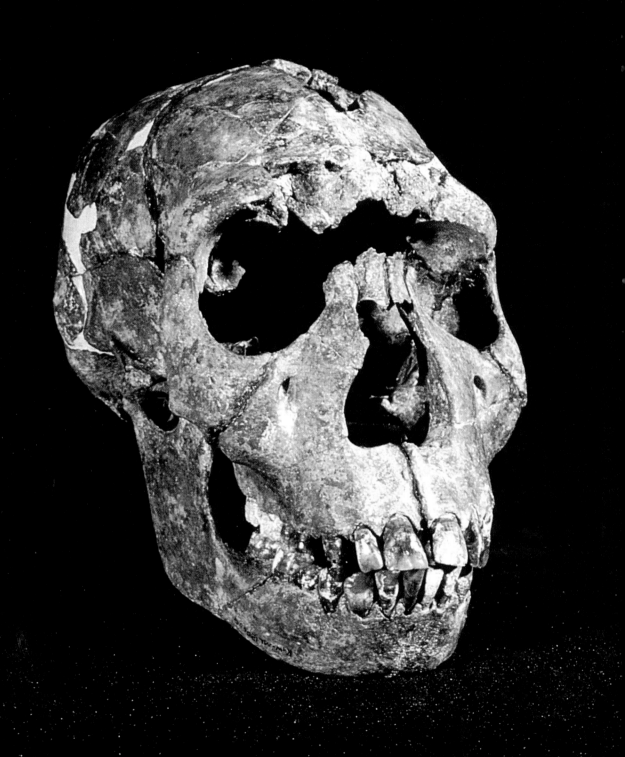

STONES AND BONES!

How Archaeologists Trace Human Origins

Prepared by Geography Department

Runestone Press ◆ Minneapolis

RUNESTONE PRESS • ᚱᚢᚾᚻᛏᚻᛏᚻᛏ

rune (rōōn) *n* **1 a :** one of the earliest written alphabets used in northern Europe, dating back to A.D. 200; **b :** an alphabet character believed to have magic powers; **c :** a charm; **d :** an Old Norse or Finnish poem. **2 :** a poem or incantation of mysterious significance, often carved in stone.

Stones and Bones! How Archaeologists Trace Human Origins is a fully revised and updated edition of *Introducing Prehistory,* a title previously published by Lerner Publications Company. The text is completely reset in 12/15 Albertus, and new photographs and captions have been added.

Thanks to Dr. Guy Gibbon, Department of Anthropology, University of Minnesota, for his help in preparing this book.

Words in **bold** type are listed in a glossary that starts on page 60.

Library of Congress Cataloging–in–Publication Data

Stones and bones!: how archaeologists trace human origins / prepared by Geography Department, Runestone Press.
    p. cm—(Buried Worlds)
Includes index.
Summary: Describes how our prehistoric ancestors may have lived and how archaeologists find and study the remains of early humans.
    ISBN 0–8225–3207–7 (lib. bdg.)
    1. Archaeology—Methodology—Juvenile literature. 2. Man—Origin—Juvenile literature. [1. Archaeology. 2. Man, Prehistoric. 3. Man—Origin.]
I. Title. II. Series.
CC75.R66 1994
930.1'028—dc20   93–2480
   CIP
                                                                  AC

Manufactured in the United States of America
1 2 3 4 5 6 – I/JR – 99 98 97 96 95 94

CONTENTS

WHAT IS PREHISTORY?

When we talk about the history of humans, we are usually referring to the lives of people who existed during the past 5,000 years. Many of these people left behind written records of their hopes, fears, beliefs, and achievements. As a result, this 5,000-year period is sometimes called the time of recorded history. From these writings, historians have learned a great deal about how people lived and worked in ancient times.

Because we often depend on written records for information, we sometimes do not realize how far-reaching human history is. We may think that humans originated in the fertile river valleys of the Middle East, among the temples of ancient China, or in the early walled cities of the Americas.

To scientists, these civilizations represent only the most recent history of the human species, which actually began on the grassy plains of eastern Africa about five million years ago. The vast span of time before recorded history is known as **prehistory**.

It's Been a Long Time

The history of civilization often repeats itself. Scholars who study written records have found familiar patterns of growth, prosperity, and decline or of war, revolution, and conquest. But the 5,000-year history of civilization represents only a tiny fraction of the human story.

To get a better idea of how short recorded history is when compared to prehistory, imagine that this book symbolizes five million years, with each page representing an equal number of years. As you turn the pages of the book, you march through time, seeing small bands of hunters and gatherers who moved their camps from place to place. Although these wanderers would eventually develop strong weapons and sturdy dwellings, their basic way of life would change little until the last page of the book.

About halfway down the last page, humans would begin to farm the land and to settle in permanent villages. In the last two or three sentences, people would build the first cities and invent writing. These last sentences represent recorded history, a time that we know in detail. The pages leading up to this point make up prehistory.

A prehistoric artist engraved this image of a buffalo into a bone about 15,000 years ago. Archaeologists (scientists who dig up and study ancient objects) unearthed the artwork in France.

Prehistorians

Scientists who dig up and study the remains of ancient humans are called **archaeologists**. Their job is to locate old cities, houses, graves, tools, and other **artifacts**, whether they are buried in the desert, hidden in tombs, or lying on the ocean floor.

Most archaeologists study the remains of people who lived either in cities or in permanent villages. These early settlers left behind graves, workshops, public buildings, temples, and common tools and weapons. Over a long period of time, these possessions accumulated in layers, or **strata**. When archaeologists discover an ancient city, they often find artifacts from different periods embedded in the strata.

A special group of archaeologists—called **paleoanthropologists**—studies prehistoric remains. This specialization combines the expertise of anthropologists, who

An Australian paleoanthropologist (a scientist who specializes in studying prehistoric human remains) examines rock paintings crafted by Aborigines about 11,000 B.C. Australia's earliest inhabitants, the Aborigines migrated to the continent from Asia about 35,000 years ago.

A digger carefully removes stones from a site in the United States. Close study of these rocks may reveal that prehistoric peoples shaped the stones into tools or weapons.

study human culture, and paleontologists, who study fossils. Fossils are the hardened remains or the imprints of prehistoric plants and animals left in the earth.

A Guessing Game

Paleoanthropologists deal with wandering groups that hunted and gathered their food. These early humans rarely stayed in one place for very long and seldom left behind any belongings. For this reason, paleoanthropologists must be good detectives. They must try to guess the movements of human beings who lived thousands or even millions of years ago.

The search for evidence of prehistoric life has only just begun.

Paleontologists (scientists who study the remains of plants and animals) discovered these fossilized (hardened) remains of a prehistoric fish swallowing a smaller fish.

Although paleoanthropologists have been working for about 150 years, most of the world is yet to be investigated. These archaeologists have focused on eastern Africa, central Asia, Europe, and North America. Most of prehistoric Africa, Asia, South America, and Australia are still unexplored territory.

A paleontologist examines prehistoric animal bones that have been chipped out of a rock formation. Paleontologists can help archaeologists determine what types of plants and animals lived at the same time as prehistoric humans.

EUGÈNE DUBOIS'S SEARCH FOR THE MISSING LINK

In the nineteenth century, most people believed that modern animals evolved from prehistoric species. But the idea that humans could have evolved from earlier beings, such as prehistoric apes, was not widely accepted. Eugène Dubois, a Dutch doctor and anthropologist, was a strong believer in human evolution. In the late 1800s, he set out to find the fossils (hardened bones of prehistoric animals) that would provide the missing link between humans and apes.

Dubois believed that the earliest humans probably lived in the warm, lush climate of the tropics. In 1887, after he failed to find financial support for an anthropological expedition to this area, Dubois entered the Dutch army as a doctor. The army sent him to Sumatra, a tropical island in Southeast Asia that was then under Dutch rule.

In 1890 the army transferred Dubois to the neighboring island of Java. With the help of a small excavation crew, Dubois began systematically to search for fossils. After months of digging, workers uncovered part of a stone-encrusted skull, a thighbone, and a tooth. Convinced that these finds represented the missing link between apes and humans, Dubois named his find *Pithecanthropus erectus,* meaning "the apeman that walked erect." The remains are better known as Java Man.

Despite the evidence, most of Dubois's colleagues doubted that he had found the missing link, and modern experts agree with this conclusion. Dubois's belief in human evolution and his thorough excavation methods, however, inspired other scientists to continue the search for the missing link.

Eugène Dubois was one of the first scientists to dig for prehistoric human fossils.

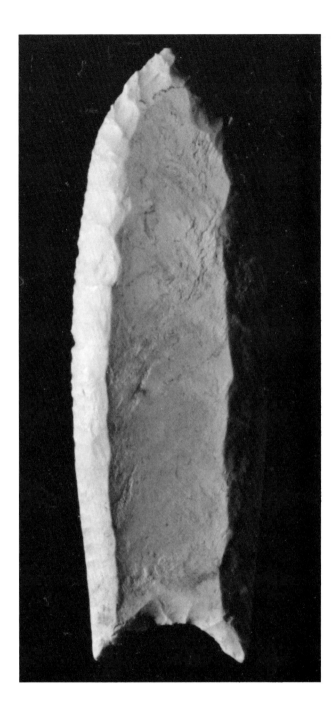

A prehistoric weapon maker probably made this stone point by striking its edges with another rock or with a piece of wood or bone.

Since prehistoric people lived so long ago, most of their possessions have disappeared. Their wood, leather, and bone objects quickly rotted and broke up in the soil. Stone, however, is very durable and can hold the same shape for thousands of years when buried in the ground. Therefore, it is mostly through stone tools that archaeologists have learned about the lives and activities of prehistoric humans.

Because archaeologists have so little evidence, most of their knowledge of prehistoric people is guesswork. As scientists explore more of the world for prehistoric remains, they will probably discover that some of these guesses were wrong. Scientists often change their conclusions about the lives of early humans, and we cannot assume that current theories about our prehistoric ancestors are accurate.

Prehistoric people left behind no written records and very few objects. As a result, paleoanthropologists can only guess what languages these early humans spoke, what poems and stories they told, what kinds of laws and customs they lived by, and what gods and spirits they believed in. But by studying their bones, their stone tools, their artwork, and the remains of their dwellings, archaeologists can offer clues about how the earliest humans lived.

Early hunters used sharpened stones attached to sticks to spear large animals— such as the mastodon, the ancestor of the elephant.

DIGGING
UP THE PAST

Although prehistoric people are often thought of as cave dwellers, only a small fraction of them actually lived in caves. Most early humans roamed in the open, building temporary shelters near lakes, rivers, or forests. These wanderers probably chose sites that provided an abundance of wild plants, game, water, and natural protection from enemies.

Buried Clues

Archaeologists find most prehistoric objects buried in the ground, but sometimes an artifact is found lying on the surface in plain sight. Such objects are usually badly damaged by long exposure to wind and rain, which can wear away evidence of prehistoric life. But surface finds often indicate that many more prehistoric remains are nearby.

When archaeologists find a prehistoric object on the surface, they carefully mark the spot. They can then return to the site to **excavate** (dig). Archaeologists work slowly and carefully, removing the soil with tools as small as paintbrushes and dental picks.

Archaeological excavation is a difficult, time-consuming, and costly operation that frequently requires the combined efforts of a large team of experts and workers. For example, excavators often include natural scientists, such as geologists, botanists, and zoologists. They examine the soil, search for evidence of past climates, and study the plant and animal life.

After prehistoric remains have been excavated, they are taken to archaeological laboratories and carefully studied. Eventually, the paleoanthropologist will write a report—or perhaps a series of reports—about the remains.

These reports are published in scientific journals and are read by hundreds of other archaeologists all over the world. They compare the

An excavator employs small tools to dig around stones on a prehistoric site. A recorder will chart the exact location of the rocks before they are removed. Later study of the chart may reveal that early people arranged the stones to form a wall or a fireplace.

new information with the results of their own work. In this way, archaeologists work together to develop a clear picture of how prehistoric humans lived.

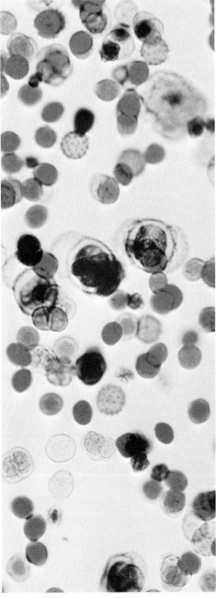

Tiny pollen grains found in the soil can offer archaeologists clues to what types of plants existed in prehistoric times.

The Prehistoric Environment

Archaeologists study two different types of prehistoric remains. One kind includes objects that are directly connected to the humans that once lived on a site. These remains include bones, skulls, teeth, tools, weapons, and traces of human dwellings, such as walls, fireplaces, storage pits, or smooth dirt floors. The other type of study explores the site's natural environment by digging up the remains of plants and animals found deep in the soil.

Such remains would not be important if the environment remained the same as time passes. But the earth's climate is constantly changing. With the passage of thousands or millions of years, regions that were once covered with forests may gradually turn into grasslands. Marshes may dry up and turn into deserts. Large areas of the earth's surface may become submerged beneath the sea, while other regions once submerged may become dry land.

In some periods, the earth has grown cold, and great sheets of ice from the polar regions have moved over warmer lands, crushing everything in their path. At other times, the earth has been warmed, and vast areas of land have turned into steamy, swampy jungles. Tall mountain ranges have gradually eroded away and become gently

A slow-moving glacier (sheet of ice) in Antarctica left behind this deep swirl on a snow-packed hill (left). Thousands of years ago, when ice covered much of North America, a glacier carved a steep canyon in Montana (right).

rounded hills. Flat land has been pushed upward by forces deep inside the earth to become jagged mountains. As the shape and temperature of the earth have changed, so have its plants and animals.

Over thousands of years, the environment can change several times at any one location. For this reason, scientists cannot know exactly what the environment was like on a prehistoric site simply by studying the environment that exists there today. They must also examine natural prehistoric remains.

Animal bones, for example, show what species inhabited that region long ago. Even broken animal bones tell a story. By studying the way that bones have been broken, archaeologists can sometimes determine which animals were eaten by prehistoric people. Archaeologists can also identify plant remains, especially seeds and pollen, both of which can survive in the soil for thousands of years.

Search and Destroy

When archaeologists begin excavating a site, they assume a heavy responsibility. To search for ancient objects, they must destroy the site. Modern methods of excavation, however, ensure that no object will be overlooked. As diggers remove soil, they pass it through strainers to catch small objects like teeth, beads, or tiny pieces of bone. All remains are removed and set aside, and the leftover soil, gravel, and rock is piled in a heap.

Archaeologists keep complete records of the excavation. Some workers take photographs and make maps and charts that show different types of soil at different levels. Other excavators note the exact location and position of each artifact.

Using these methods, archaeologists can go back and check the records if they need information that may not have seemed important during the excavation. For example, diggers might remove stones that do not seem to have any special meaning but will record the exact position of each stone as it is removed. Later, when the positions of all the stones are drawn on a map, the picture may suddenly reveal that some of the rocks were buried in a straight line or in a circle. This discovery could indicate that the stones were part of a wall or a fireplace.

All archaeologists follow these excavation methods, but paleo-anthropologists are particularly meticulous. The objects that these scientists search for are much smaller and more difficult to find than the tombs, temples, cities, and pyramids that other archaeologists may be seeking. After sifting all the excavated soil through a screen, the paleoanthropologist mixes it with water and strains it again, in case the remains of insects, seeds, or microorganisms escaped the first sifting.

Analyzing Prehistoric Remains

After prehistoric remains are removed from a site, they are often taken to laboratories to be analyzed. There, chemical tests, microscopic examinations, and other scientific techniques provide information about the objects that cannot be gained by observation alone.

For instance, scientists can analyze the remains of ancient fireplaces to determine what materials prehistoric people burned. Wood, fat, oils, and manure—all of which were used by prehistoric people as fuel—leave certain residues that can be identified by laboratory analysis. Through examination of the stones that line a prehistoric fireplace, lab workers can also determine how hot a fire was. Because cooking fires need to be much hotter than fires lit for warmth and light, archaeologists can learn how prehistoric fireplaces were used.

Animal bones discovered in fireplaces are valuable finds. From examination, paleoanthropologists can often tell not only what animals prehistoric people had for dinner but how much meat they ate. When this information is combined with the analysis of seeds and pollen, archaeologists can reconstruct a reasonably accurate picture of the past environments of a particular site.

How Old is "Old"?

Knowing the age of an object helps paleoanthropologists to determine not only how long the artifact has

Archaeologists in China carefully scrape dirt from the skull of an early human.

The depth of colored strata—or layers—found on an excavation site can help archaeologists determine which objects are older and which are younger.

been buried in the ground but also who used it and what its purpose was. Objects from the last 5,000 years sometimes contain clues to their age—writing, for example, or the image of a known historical ruler. But objects left by prehistoric people contain no such indications. For this reason, paleoanthropologists must rely on other kinds of information to date a prehistoric object.

The most common method of dating is based on the study of strata. Because each new stratum lies on top of a previous stratum, the higher strata are newer than those on the bottom. Thus, when an archaeologist excavates a site, the lower strata are assumed to be the oldest.

By studying these layers, archaeologists can learn which objects on a site are older and which are younger, according to their depth

in the excavation site. But archaeologists cannot pinpoint what year an object was made from its placement. For a precise age, scientists must use other methods.

One of the most accurate laboratory methods is carbon-14 dating. This technique relies on the fact that all living organisms absorb the radioactive material carbon 14 at a known rate. After an organism dies, the carbon 14 contained in the organism is gradually converted to carbon 12. This conversion also happens at a known rate. By measuring how much carbon 14 is left in the remains, archaeologists can determine when plants and animals died.

Carbon-14 dating is very useful in analyzing charred wood and pieces of bone from prehistoric fireplaces. When these materials are blackened by fire, they are less likely to rot and disappear into the

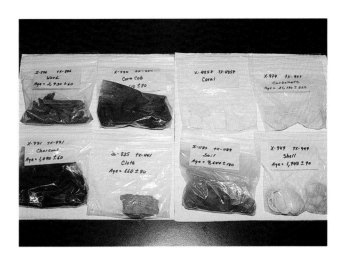

During an excavation, archaeologists collect samples of once-living materials. Laboratory scientists can determine the age of these samples using the carbon-14 dating method.

soil, and most of the carbon 14 still remains to be measured. In this case, scientists can use the carbon-14 dating method to discover when a prehistoric fire was made.

Remains more than 50,000 years old, however, have lost almost all traces of carbon 14 and cannot be dated with this method. But scientists have discovered that other

A lab worker carefully prepares a charcoal sample for carbon dating.

Paleoanthropologist Donald Johanson displays the skeletal remains of Lucy, a prehistoric human who lived about 3.5 million years ago.

LOVELY LUCY

In 1974 a U.S. paleoanthropologist named Donald Johanson led a fossil-hunting expedition to Hadar, Ethiopia. As he headed back to camp from a fossil site, Johanson noticed a small, brown bone lying in a gully. Close inspection revealed that the object was a prehistoric arm bone. As he looked around, Johanson noticed other bones in the area and wondered if they all belonged to the same human.

The find proved to be remarkable, for Johanson had uncovered the remains of the earliest known type of humanlike animal, *Australopithecus afarensis.* He nicknamed his discovery Lucy after the popular song "Lucy in the Sky with Diamonds."

Experts believe Lucy lived about 3.5 million years ago. Her bone structure reveals that she walked upright and stood about 3.5 feet (107 centimeters) tall. She was about 19 years old when she died. From the shape of her skull, scientists believe Lucy's features were more apelike than humanlike. Although she had a small brain, the rest of her body resembled a modern human.

The year after finding Lucy, Johanson discovered numerous bones belonging to 13 more prehistoric humans, all of whom he believed were members of *Australopithecus afarensis.* Together, Lucy and the fellow members of her species have provided important clues to early human life.

radioactive substances change even more slowly.

A radioactive form of the element potassium—known as potassium 40—changes into the gas argon at a known rate. Scientists can measure this slow transformation to date volcanic rocks that formed millions of years ago. By using the potassium-argon method to date volcanic rocks found near prehistoric objects, archaeologists can determine an approximate date for a prehistoric stratum.

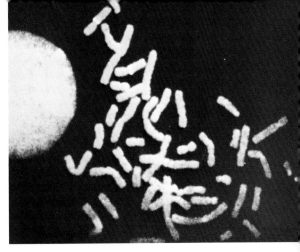

Scientists can study chromosomes (above) from present-day beings to learn when two species—such as humans and apes—once shared a common ancestor.

The DNA Record

In recent years, scientists have begun to study human history by examining modern **cells**—the building blocks of all living things. Every cell contains deoxyribonucleic acid (DNA). DNA is a chemical substance in the **genes** of living things. Genes, which determine appearance, gender, and other features, are located in **chromosomes**, the threadlike structures in the center of cells. As the human body grows, its cells divide, an action that duplicates chromosomes and genes and passes them on to all new cells.

Sometimes changes occur during the duplicating process, and the chromosomes are not copied exactly. These differences between the original chromosomes and the duplicates are called **mutations.** Through tests, scientists can predict the average number of mutations that will occur in the chromosomes of a specific **species** (kind of living thing) over a long period of time.

Many scientific tests have compared apes and humans—two species of **primates** that share a common ancestor. Scientists believe that the chromosomes of apes and humans were once the same. Even today, the chromosomes of these two species are 99 percent identical.

By comparing a cell from a modern ape with a cell from a modern human, scientists can count the number of differences between the two sets of chromosomes. This comparison has led scientists to report that the common ancestor of these primates lived about five million years ago. At that time, mutations in the chromosomes of this ancestor began dividing apes and humans into two different species.

23

THE PRIMATE FAMILY

For centuries, people accepted the biblical concept that humans were created separately from all other living things. But some revolutionary scientific discoveries during the nineteenth century cast doubt on these traditional ideas about the origin of our species.

New Ideas

In 1856 archaeologists unearthed the remains of an unusual skeleton in Germany's Neander Gorge. The bones did not come from any known ape, monkey, or other living species of animal. The skeleton —especially the skull—was almost the same as that of a human.

In time, scientists concluded that the bones were indeed from a human, but a human very different from modern people. Scientists named this specimen Neanderthal. Since the discovery of the first Neanderthal remains, archaeologists have found the skulls and bones of Neanderthal men, women, and children at more than 40 different sites.

Another important event occurred just three years later, when Charles Darwin published *The Origin of Species*. In this book, Darwin proposed his theory of evolution. This theory explained how many animal species gradually change, or evolve, with the passage of time to become new

A young chimpanzee rests near its mother. The animals most closely related to humans, chimpanzees can make simple tools and use signals to communicate.

species. Scholars, scientists, and religious leaders argued bitterly about Darwin's theories, but most people eventually came to accept the idea of evolution.

These two events helped change how people think about humanity. Darwin's work supported the idea that plants and animals had not been suddenly created but had gradually evolved from other species. The Neanderthal skeleton showed that a different type of human once lived on the earth.

Most anthropologists believe that modern humans evolved from some form of **archaic *sapiens,*** the subspecies to which Neanderthals belong. Archaic *sapiens* probably evolved from still other types of prehistoric peoples.

Similar but Different

Humans evolved from other animals, but we are more than just another species. We have accom-

In his theory of evolution, Charles Darwin explained how plants and animals—including humans—may have slowly evolved from other species.

plished things that no other animals have even tried, from building fires to landing on the moon. These unique traits make our minds and bodies different from all other forms of life.

Although great differences exist between humans and other animals, there are also some similarities. For example, some other animals make tools, communicate with each other, teach their young how to behave, and use logic in solving problems. At one time, scientists believed that only humans could do such things. But careful studies of the behavior of monkeys and apes in the wild have revealed that these traits are shared by some of our nearest relatives in the animal kingdom.

Tools, Chimpanzees, and Logic

Scientists once believed that animals acted only according to instinct, while humans used logic and learning. But we now know that more complex animals, such as dogs, porpoises, monkeys, and apes, have to learn such basic things as what kinds of foods to eat and how to greet each other. Chimpanzees, for example, learn different forms of greeting. Some chimpanzees touch one another's hips, while others touch hands. When two groups of chimpanzees meet, they make noises that sound like a wild party.

The ability to make tools was once considered the most basic difference between humans and other animals. But British scientist Jane Goodall, who began studying chimpanzees in 1960, discovered that these animals also make tools. The chimpanzees' tools are inspired by their appetite for termites.

Because termite nests are as hard as concrete, chimpanzees cannot easily get at the insects inside. But chimpanzees learned to capture termites by inserting a stick into the nest. Termites swarm to the stick, and the chimpanzee then pulls it out and licks off the termites. To make these tools, a chimpanzee first selects a thin twig from a tree, strips off the leaves, and breaks it to the correct length.

Scientists call this termite stick a tool because the chimpanzee must perform many different actions before eating the termites. The success of the termite search shows that chimpanzees can make plans and work intelligently toward a goal. The animals, for example, may form the idea of eating termites, although a termite nest may not be in sight. Mental abilities such as these are rare among animals.

Scientists originally thought that monkeys and apes ate only readily available food, such as insects, snails, or birds' eggs. But field studies have shown that some apes—especially chimpanzees—actually hunt and eat other animals.

27

Like humans, chimpanzees make tools. This chimpanzee uses a stick to harvest termites from their hard nests.

They even cooperate in hunting wild game and share the meat if the hunt is successful. The basic human activities of cooperative hunting and food sharing were once believed to be unknown among apes and monkeys.

The capacities to learn and to make tools are some of the characteristics that humans share with other animals. Yet there is a vast difference between the human ability to make a spacecraft or a computer and the chimpanzee's ability to make a termite stick. Although other animals can do many of the things we do, there is much more that they cannot do. But it is important to be aware of the similarities between people and animals, because these common abilities help us to understand how our own capabilities evolved.

Standing Upright

About five million years ago, when our apelike ancestors adopted a fully erect posture and began to travel on their hind legs, they started on the evolutionary road that led to modern humans. These very first humans had small brains, and they probably looked more like apes than like people.

In contrast to the short, stubby hind legs of most apes and monkeys, the hind legs of early humans were strong and slender. These streamlined limbs were well suited for running and walking long distances. They also enabled humans to develop the use of their forelimbs, or arms. With their arms free, early people could throw dangerous weapons, make tools, and carry objects.

JANE GOODALL: CHAMPION OF THE CHIMPANZEES

As a child living in England, Jane Goodall was fascinated by animals. At the age of 7 she read *The Story of Doctor Dolittle,* a book about a man who could talk to animals, including African chimpanzees. From that time on, she longed to work with chimpanzees, and at the age of 23 she boarded a plane for Africa. Goodall was eventually hired as an assistant to the famed paleoanthropologist Louis Leakey. He offered her a chance to study chimpanzees in northern Tanzania's Gombe National Park.

Through daily contact with the chimpanzees, Goodall won their trust. She observed the animals at close range and wrote detailed reports of their behavior. She discovered that chimpanzees eat not only fruits and nuts, as scientists then believed, but also hunt other animals. In addition, Goodall learned that chimpanzees use tools and form groups that make war on each other. After more than 30 years of observation, Goodall has become one of the world's foremost experts on the behavior of our closest animal relatives.

In recent years, Goodall has worked to protect the world's dwindling population of chimpanzees. Destruction of forest habitats and poaching (illegal hunting) have reduced the number of these animals. Through her lectures and writings, Goodall hopes to raise awareness of the problem and to save the animals she believes are a bridge between us and the rest of the animal world.

Since the first humans lacked the powerful teeth and claws of their apelike ancestors, they had no natural weapons with which to defend themselves. For this reason, they fashioned weapons out of wood and stone.

Erect posture, the full use of hands and arms, and the lack of strong teeth and claws led early humans to ensure their survival in new ways. While other animals might have relied on their strength and speed, humans survived by making things with their hands.

This activity required a strong intellect and the ability to think and plan. In time, these skills became numerous, and the human brain processed more and more information. As a result, the human brain gradually grew to twice its original size. The increase in human skills, thought processes, and other examples of intelligence created a way of life based mainly on learning rather than on instinct. This system of learning how to live is called a **culture**.

Within a culture, people share traditions, beliefs, inventions, and language. Through the use of language, humans can share their experiences, cooperate with each other, and teach their offspring the culture of the group. In this way, language, learning, and culture are all connected, forming a distinctively human way of life not shared by any other species.

Language and Learning

Physical differences in the vocal organs and in the language area of the brain prevent monkeys and apes from speaking. Some apes, however, have the capacity to communicate using hand or body signals. Yet unlike humans, who use language, monkeys and apes do not use their signals to share the ideas and beliefs of a common culture.

Human brains are constructed in a way that enables us to form ideas about events that are not actually happening. We can imagine what it might be like to do something in the future, in a different time and place. We can also imagine certain qualities of things without imagining the things themselves. For example, we do not have to imagine a red apple or a loud clap of thunder to form the ideas of redness or loudness.

Human children begin to think in this manner as they learn words that represent thoughts and ideas. We can use these words to communicate with other people. No other animal is able to use sounds to represent such abstract ideas.

Humans mature more slowly than almost any other animal. In the 15 or 20 years it takes us to reach adulthood, dogs, cats, goats, sheep, cows, pigs, monkeys, and many other animals live out their natural lives and die of old age.

Prehistoric hunters prepare to drop heavy rocks on a family of bears. Since humans have no natural weapons, such as claws or sharp teeth, early people learned to hunt and to defend themselves with weapons.

During the many years of childhood, our brains grow larger and larger. The brains of a human infant and a newborn chimpanzee are about the same size. But while the chimpanzee's brain will increase about 25 percent as the animal grows up, the human's brain will increase about 400 percent. For this reason, there is room in the human brain for acquiring new kinds of information throughout an average lifespan.

A baby chimpanzee is strong and quick within only a few days of its birth, and within a few weeks it begins to look for its own food. But a human baby is helpless for months and can take care of itself only after many years. This long period of adult protection allows humans to absorb far more information than other animals. By the time humans reach adulthood, they know much more than the wisest gorilla or chimpanzee.

THE FIRST HUMANS

Humans were not always as different from other animals as they are today. The first humans, for example, had brains that were only slightly larger than the brains of the chimpanzee, our smartest ape relative. Early humans used simple tools and stood erect, but in most other respects they lived very much like other animals.

Australopithecus

Paleoanthropologists believe that the first humanlike animal lived in southeastern Africa from more than five million years ago to about one million years ago. This early human—which scientists named **Australopithecus** (meaning "southern ape")—stood upright and walked on two legs.

The first *Australopithecus* remains were discovered in 1924 by Raymond Dart, an Australian anthropologist. While going through a box of bones found at Taung, South Africa, Dart came upon a child's skull. He believed that the skull belonged to an early human. Although many scientists thought the Taung Baby was an ape, the discovery of similar remains in other areas of Africa eventually proved Dart's idea.

Scientists have identified four different species of *Australopithecines. Australopithecus afarensis* and *Australopithecus africanus* were small-boned and reached only about 4 feet (122 centimeters) in height. *Australopithecus boisei* and *Australopithecus robustus* were massively built and stood about 5 feet (152 cm) tall.

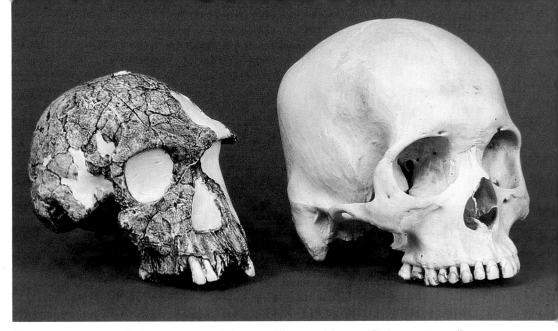

The reconstructed skull of **Australopithecus africanus** *(above left)* **is much smaller than the skull of a modern human** *(above right)*. **Most scientists believe that present-day people evolved from this small-boned human. The shape of a hardened** Australopithecus *footprint* *(below)* **indicates that these first humans walked erect.**

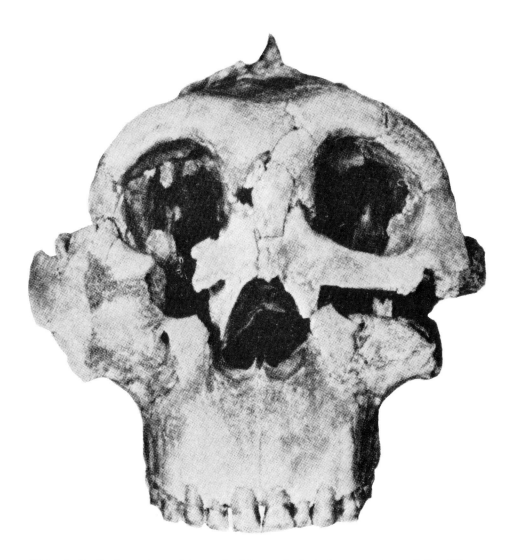

This skull of a large-boned Australopithecus boisei *dates to about 1.8 million years ago.*

Most paleoanthropologists believe that modern humans evolved from the smaller *Australopithecines.*

The First Toolmakers

The earliest *Australopithecines* had brains about one-third the size of those of modern humans. Gradu-ally, the size and intellectual capacity of this brain increased. Some scientists believe that the larger brain size of later *Australopithecines* enabled these early humans to make very simple stone tools by about two million years ago.

Prehistoric people made their tools from large, round stones. When toolmakers struck these rocks with other stones, large chips called **flakes** fell from the sides, leaving a jagged tool. Although these tools were very simple, they were capable of chopping open a dead animal or of cutting through branches and the tough roots of edible plants.

The first prehistoric tools—called pebble tools—were small, sharpened stones that probably served as cutters and scrapers. By about 1.5 million years ago, people began to make chopping tools. Eventually, humans also started employing flake tools with very sharp edges.

It may seem that some of these tools could simply be stones that were naturally broken into tool shapes. But certain signs help scientists distinguish real stone tools from pieces of broken rock. When a toolmaker deliberately hits one stone with another, the resulting break is quite different from the natural crack in a rock.

Prehistoric toolmakers fashioned tools from large, round stones called cores.

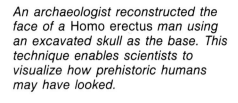

An archaeologist reconstructed the face of a Homo erectus *man using an excavated skull as the base. This technique enables scientists to visualize how prehistoric humans may have looked.*

FACES FROM THE PAST

When paleoanthropologists uncover the remains of a prehistoric human, they can examine the bone structure to determine its origin. But they can usually only imagine how the living person may have looked. Some archaeologists, however, are also artists who specialize in putting faces on prehistoric skulls.

Over time, scientists have developed standard measurements for the thickness of skin on different parts of the face. These measurements are based on age, gender, and ethnic background. For example, the tissue thickness on the glabella, or area between the eyebrows, is measured at .22 inches (5.5 millimeters) for a white male.

Using these measurements, artists begin recreating a prehistoric face by determining how thick to make the skin on each

part of the head. Some artists place small erasers, cut to the appropriate skin depths, at different points on the skull. Using the erasers as a guide, the artist molds clay to the skull. When the clay is spread to the right thickness, the artist can follow the contours of the face to shape features, such as the nose, the cheekbones, and the mouth. In the final stage, the artist adds lines or wrinkles to the clay skin and attaches hair to make the restored head look realistic.

This process helps archaeologists visualize prehistoric humans, but the restorations may or may not be true to life. In fact, different experts often come up with varying results, even though they all started with the same skull. By putting a face on the past, however, we can more easily imagine our ancestors living and working in prehistoric times.

When a fast-moving object strikes something hard, it produces a cone-shaped shock wave, similar to the hole made in a window by the force of a bullet. Sometimes this shock wave also has small ripples in it, like the ripples formed on the surface of a quiet pond when a stone is thrown into it. Archaeologists examine stones excavated from archaeological sites for the small, conelike bumps and the ring-shaped ripples of shock waves. These patterns are almost never produced naturally, because rocks usually wear down too slowly for shock waves to form.

How They Lived

Australopithecines survived by gathering plant foods, such as fruits, nuts, and roots. They also hunted small animals, including antelopes and pigs, as well as frogs, reptiles, and small rodents. In their work, excavators have unearthed few remains of large animals—like elephants, hippopotamuses, and giraffes—among the stones and bones of the first humans. As a result, many scientists believe that the earliest people lacked the skills and weapons to hunt large game.

Australopithecines hunted small animals, such as antelopes, which thrived on the tall grasses of the African savanna.

Australopithecines *probably built temporary shelters made of wood or grass on the vast plains of eastern Africa, where acacia trees are a common sight.*

Unlike their ape ancestors, who moved constantly, the first humans probably occupied their homes for days or weeks at a time. They left during the day to hunt and gather food and returned at night to sleep in the safety of their groups. Humans probably brought much of their food back to their camp to share with others. Among chimpanzees, adult males do almost all of the hunting, and the same was probably true of the first humans. While the men hunted, women most likely gathered plants.

Apes usually wandered about in groups, sleeping wherever they happened to be when night fell. When apes found food, they sat down and ate it on the spot. Thus, while they usually slept near each other at night, apes did not have a home base in the sense that early humans did.

Most *Australopithecines* lived in eastern Africa. They settled near lake shores and along rivers, where animals came to drink. Africa's vast plains offered the first humans an abundance of small wild game. Nearby forests provided shelter and a variety of plant foods.

Even at this early stage of human development, people were learning how to live in groups. As their skills and intelligence grew, they developed more complex societies that used simple languages and customs. At the same time, humans began to mature more slowly, giving children more time to learn how to fit into their society and how to survive in the world.

HUNTERS AND FIRE BUILDERS

During excavations in 1960 at Olduvai Gorge in the eastern African nation of Tanzania, British anthropologist Mary Leakey discovered human remains. The bones differed greatly from the bones of *Australopithecus*. This new human species, which many scientists believe evolved from the *Australopithecus* about two million years ago, was named **Homo habilis**, a Latin name meaning "skillful human being."

In 1987 more excavations at Olduvai Gorge produced skull, arm, and thigh bones of *Homo habilis*. From these remains, paleoanthropologists concluded that *Homo habilis* had a larger brain than *Australopithecus* had. Although little more than half the size of a modern human brain, this enlarged brain enabled *Homo habilis* to create better formed stone tools.

Between 1.5 million and 300,000 years ago, *Homo habilis* evolved into **Homo erectus**, meaning "upright human being." Changes in the shape of the pelvis bone, to which legs are attached, and a greater arch in the foot gave *Homo erectus* a more even weight distribution. As a result, *Homo erectus* was the first human who could walk upright for lengthy periods of time without strain. *Homo erectus* traveled long distances, migrating eastward across Asia and northward into Europe.

The low, sloping forehead and large jaw of a **Homo erectus** *skull (right) are highlighted in an artist's reconstruction of the prehistoric human (below).*

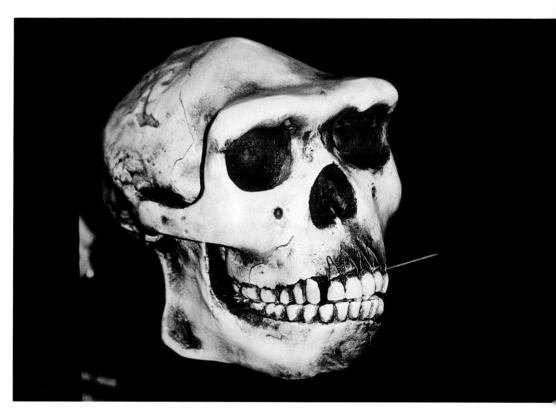

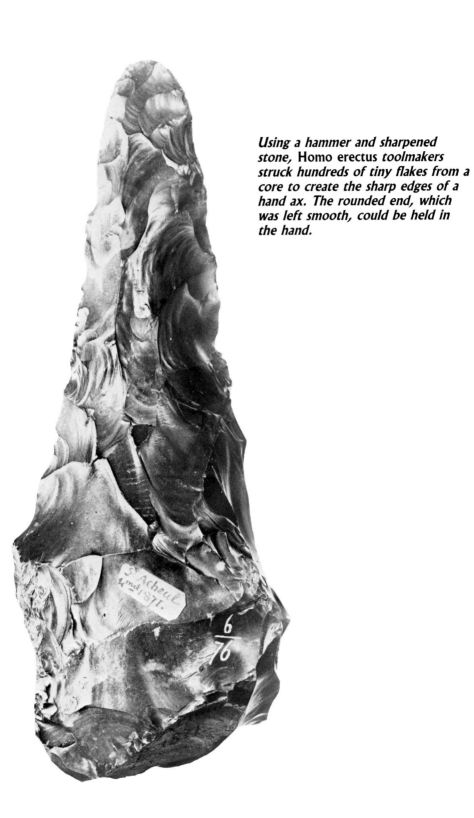

Using a hammer and sharpened stone, Homo erectus *toolmakers struck hundreds of tiny flakes from a core to create the sharp edges of a hand ax. The rounded end, which was left smooth, could be held in the hand.*

Homo erectus

The members of *Homo erectus* were not built like their ancestors, nor did they resemble modern humans either. Although their bodies looked much like ours do, their heavy, thick bones required more supportive muscle. A key difference between *Homo erectus* and a modern human is the shape of the skull. Members of *Homo erectus* had low, sloping foreheads and very large jaws. Over time, however, their brains expanded, making their foreheads more rounded.

A larger, more complex brain distinguished members of *Homo erectus* from their ancestors. An increased intelligence also enabled *Homo erectus* to create more advanced tools and weapons than *Homo habilis* could. Archaeologists have unearthed many *Homo erectus* axes shaped like pears, with a sharp point at the top and a rounded bottom that could be held in the hand.

At first, *Homo erectus* made these simple hand axes in a variety of shapes and sizes. As time went on, hand axes became increasingly similar and more finely made. *Homo erectus* toolmakers chipped off between 100 and 200 flakes to make each hand ax. In contrast, the earliest toolmakers struck only about 10 flakes per tool.

In addition to hand axes, *Homo erectus* invented stone tools that *Australopithecus* had never even attempted. These tools included a variety of scrapers and knives, awls for boring holes, hammers, and special flake tools for working with wood, bone, and leather. Many of these tools were made by striking a stone with a wooden hammer rather than with another stone. This technique produced a softer impact, which allowed the resulting flakes to be removed more precisely.

The Hunt

Greater intelligence and better toolmaking and weapon-making skills led to more successful hunts. Members of *Homo erectus* were efficient hunters who had the patience to lie in wait for their prey. Increased intelligence also enabled these humans to use a simple language to communicate with other members of their groups. Communication allowed the hunters to make plans, such as how to encircle large animals.

While the earliest humans were content to kill small pigs and antelopes for food, members of *Homo erectus* learned to hunt larger beasts, such as giraffes, elephants, wild cattle, and giant baboons. Hunters even pursued the fearsome saber-toothed tiger, a lion-sized animal with very long, sharp teeth. Scientists who study

Although the long, sharp teeth of the saber-toothed tiger (left) and the enormous tusks of the elephant (below) were dangerous, members of Homo erectus *learned to hunt the animals successfully.*

the remains of prehistoric wildlife have suggested that some of these animals were hunted to extinction by *Homo erectus* and later humans.

The Masters of Fire

Archaeologists discovered what is possibly the oldest evidence

Flames quickly destroy a forest in Africa. Early humans may have learned about fire by watching lightning strikes start forest fires.

of fire in a cave in southern France. The remains date to about 750,000 years ago, a time well after the disappearance of *Australopithecus*. Although archaeologists disagree on the date of the earliest use of fire, they believe members of *Homo erectus* were the first humans to use and control fire.

To survive, the earliest humans made improvements on the achievements of other animals. But the control of fire was not simply an improvement. It was a revolutionary achievement that separated humans from other animals. Suddenly, humans found a way to cook food, to keep warm, to ward off predators, and to create light.

The control of fire gradually changed the position of humans from equal participants in the struggle to survive in the natural world to masters of their environment. Since most animals are afraid of fire, early humans could build a fire and create a place of safety that other animals would probably not violate.

Members of *Homo erectus* also discovered that by setting fire to dry grassland, wild game could be stampeded in the direction of a steep cliff, a sticky swamp, or a group of hunters. In this way, animals could be killed easily in large numbers.

Besides providing warmth, protection from wild animals, and assistance in the hunt, fire enabled humans to cook food, an activity no other animal can do. The discovery of cooking greatly expanded

THE LUCKY LEAKEYS

For many years, most scientists were convinced that humans had evolved in eastern Asia about 500,000 years ago. Their conclusions were based on finds of bones in Java and China. But in 1959, paleoanthropologists Louis and Mary Leakey, aided by their three sons—Jonathan, Richard, and Philip—unearthed a 1.8-million-year-old skull in eastern Africa. The skull, which they named *Australopithecus boisei,* was the first of many finds that earned the family the nickname "the lucky Leakeys."

Louis Leakey, who was born and raised in Kenya, began leading fossil-hunting expeditions in eastern Africa during the 1920s. He turned up many important fossils, including the remains of a human species that he named *Homo habilis.* His work convinced scientists that humans originated in Africa.

Mary Leakey is credited with discovering the remains of *Australopithecus boisei.* She also uncovered a trail of footprints preserved in volcanic ash in Laetoli, Tanzania. These impressions, which scientists believe were made by a humanlike creature about 3.7 million years ago, are some of the oldest known human evidence.

The family's lucky streak has also touched Richard Leakey. In 1972, while excavating the Lake Turkana area in northwestern Kenya, he discovered the skull of the oldest known *Homo habilis* fossil. The remains date to about 1.9 million years ago. A 1984 expedition in the same region turned up an almost complete *Homo erectus* skeleton. Because of the work of this remarkable family of anthropologists, we have much more information about our prehistoric ancestors.

Paleoanthropologists Louis and Mary Leakey discovered many important human fossils in Africa.

This skull and reconstructed head represent later members of Homo erectus, *who gradually developed rounded foreheads and smaller jaws.*

the range of foods humans could eat. Many foods that could not be digested well when raw—especially meat—became staples in the human diet.

As the fireplace became the center of warmth, of safety, and of food, it also became the focus of group activity. All the members of the group probably gathered around the fire in the evening to discuss the day's activities, to recall past experiences, and to make plans for the next day.

The use of fire even changed the shape of the human face. Because cooked food required much less chewing than raw food, the size of human teeth gradually decreased. Thus, while the brain was expanding, causing the forehead to bulge outward, the teeth were shrinking, causing the jaw to collapse inward. These physical changes occurred over thousands of years until *Homo erectus* developed into our own species—**Homo sapiens**, or "wise human being."

PEOPLE LIKE US

Archaeologists have found few remains from the transition period between *Homo erectus* and *Homo sapiens*. The change occurred gradually at different times in different areas of the world. Scientists believe, however, that by about 200,000 years ago *Homo sapiens* had fully replaced *Homo erectus.*

Archaic *Sapiens*

Most of our knowledge of early *Homo sapiens* comes from the subspecies archaic *sapiens*. Members of this subspecies lived in Africa, Asia, and Europe from about 130,000 to 35,000 years ago. They had heavy bones, curved limbs, and powerful teeth.

Because the archaic *sapiens* skeleton looked slightly different from a modern human skeleton, paleoanthropologists originally believed that archaic *sapiens* were a separate species of human beings. But their height, erect posture, and modern-sized brain eventually convinced scientists that present-day humans and archaic *sapiens* are members of the same species.

When archaic *sapiens* spread northward into the colder regions of Europe and Asia, they proved themselves better able to cope with cold weather than any previous human species. They chose caves and rock shelters for their dwellings and used fire for warmth and cooking. But unlike earlier humans, archaic *sapiens* used animal skins for protective clothing. This was yet another revolutionary step. No other creature uses the skins of slain animals to keep warm.

Archaic *sapiens* made tools similar to those of *Homo erectus*. But these new tools were of better quality. Archaeologists believe these early *Homo sapiens* admired good handiwork, not only because it produced a better tool but also because the object was pleasing to see and to touch. These fine tools may be the first evidence of the appreciation of beauty for its own sake.

Although they continued to use the hunting methods developed by *Homo erectus*, archaic *sapiens* tended to choose one particular animal to hunt. This type of animal varied from place to place. Some archaeologists believe that this practice led to the taming of animals for a reliable supply of meat, hides, and bone.

Life after Death

Beginning about 75,000 years ago, members of archaic *sapiens* started to dig graves for their dead. They did this not to protect the living group members from disease, but to keep the deceased at home even after death.

These prehistoric graves were small, consisting only of a round hole cut into the floors of huts or

Archaeologists believe that archaic sapiens, who lived in Africa, Europe, and Asia, made their homes in caves or under rock shelters.

caves. The body was placed into this hole in a curled-up position, with the arms and legs bent. Archaeologists have also found the remains of food and tools nestled in these graves. From these finds, paleoanthropologists concluded that archaic *sapiens* believed in life after death.

Sometimes a slab of stone was placed on top of the body before the grave was covered with soil, and in many cases archaic *sapiens* smeared an entire grave site with a red earth called ocher, perhaps as part of a burial ceremony.

Cro-Magnons

In 1868 archaeologists digging in Cro-Magnon Cave near Les Eyzies,

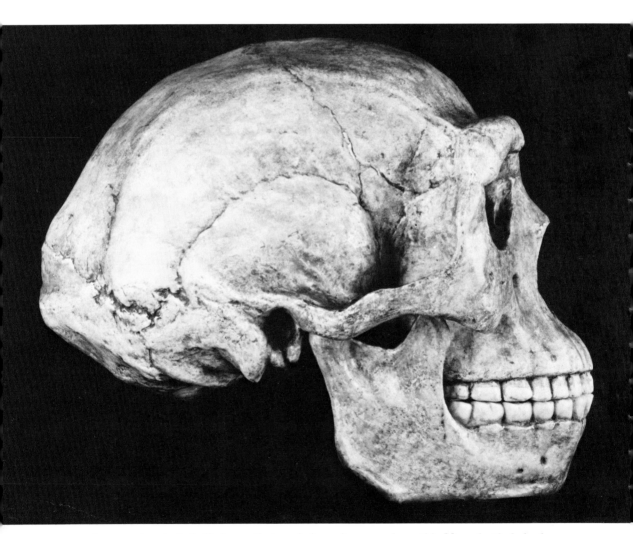

A reconstructed skull shows that archaic **sapiens,** *such as this Neanderthal, had thick bones and large, strong teeth.*

Paleoanthropologists think that archaic sapiens were the first humans to bury their dead. As an offering for the dead, antlers were placed in this grave, which dates to about 50,000 years ago.

France, discovered the bones of an early skeleton that looked much like a modern human skeleton. Since that time, more than 100 such skeletons—called **Cro-Magnons** —have been found throughout the world. Paleoanthropologists believe that Cro-Magnons were members of our subspecies—*Homo sapiens sapiens.*

Cro-Magnons probably evolved from forms of archaic *sapiens* about 35,000 years ago. Cro-Magnons lived in western Europe, but they did not look the same in all regions. Skeletons even varied

from one site to another within a certain region.

Many of these physical variations evolved because of the environment in which each group lived. For example, people who lived in cold northern climates had short thick bodies, which conserve heat better than the tall, thin bodies of settlers in warm southern regions.

About 30,000 years ago, Cro-Magnons developed the skills to create works of art. They painted pictures on rocks and on the sides of caves. Cro-Magnon artists made sculptures from stone, ivory, bone,

THE FIRST AMERICANS

Thousands of years ago, early peoples hunted and gathered food in Siberia, a region of thick forests and vast plains in present-day Russia. When hunting and gathering made animals and plants scarce in one location, the nomadic groups gradually moved eastward to new land.

The hunters eventually followed large game animals, such as bighorn bison, across a land bridge—called Beringia—that connected the continents of Asia and North America. Beringia was covered with slowly melting ice. Eventually, the ice disappeared and left the Bering Strait, a body of water that separates Russia and Alaska.

Archaeologists disagree about when people initially crossed Beringia to the Americas. Some believe that hunters arrived about 11,500 years ago and moved quickly southward, reaching South America within 500 years. Other scientists theorize that the first residents of North America journeyed across Beringia as early as 50,000 years ago and slowly migrated southward over thousands of years. More studies are needed to determine when these ancestors of Native Americans set foot in the Americas.

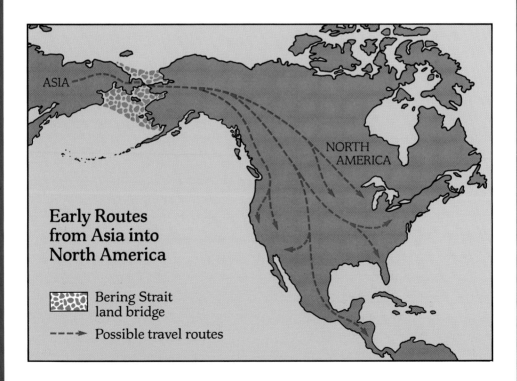

Early Routes from Asia into North America

ASIA

NORTH AMERICA

Bering Strait land bridge

- - - → Possible travel routes

Painted in black, red, and yellow colors, this image of a horse decorates Lascaux Cave in France. Archaeologists believe that Cro-Magnon artists created the picture about 15,000 years ago.

and clay. They engraved designs on rocks, bones, and antlers, and they also made jewelry. Most Cro-Magnon art depicts plants, animals, and people.

From these artworks, paleoanthropologists can determine what kinds of animals the Cro-Magnons hunted, what they ate, where they lived, and what some of their customs were. Archaeologists have also found carved symbols that may represent a simple written language.

Cro-Magnon artists specialized in crafting small statues called Venus figurines. These artworks portrayed females with full breasts, large stomachs, and small arms and legs. The Cro-Magnons probably created these figures as fertility symbols that represented a mother-goddess who gave life, kept the home, and guarded the hunt.

Precision Tools

Cro-Magnons developed new toolmaking methods to produce sophisticated stone tools. To

Excavators found this 25,000-year-old Venus figurine in eastern Europe. Cro-Magnons probably crafted these small works to represent a mother-goddess.

create axes, knives, and awls, a Cro-Magnon toolmaker placed the tip of a punch—a pointed piece of bone or antler—on a stone and struck the blunt end with a hammer. This technique caused a clean cut and allowed for great accuracy in shaping certain tools.

Some Cro-Magnons employed a technique called pressure flaking.

After heating a stone in a fire, toolmakers pressed a punchlike object on the hot stone's surface until a tiny flake popped off. In this way, small irregularities could be removed from a newly made tool, or thin flakes could be shaped into fine tools or weapons.

Using the punch, people learned to make sharp-edged blades from long, straight flakes. Using pressure flaking, blades could be shaped into knives, spear points, arrowheads, and fine tools for working in wood, bone, and ivory.

The Cro-Magnons brought their art, religion, and advanced toolmaking to many areas of the world. Their relatives migrated from Europe, Africa, and Asia to Australia, the Pacific islands, and the Americas. They learned to survive in hot deserts, in thick jungles, and in frozen polar regions. The new settlers developed their own art styles and burial customs. In fact, the distinctive stone tools of the Cro-Magnons and their relatives have helped archaeologists identify regional groups around the world.

This skull of a Cro-Magnon man looks much like the skull of a modern **Homo sapiens sapiens,** *or present-day human.*

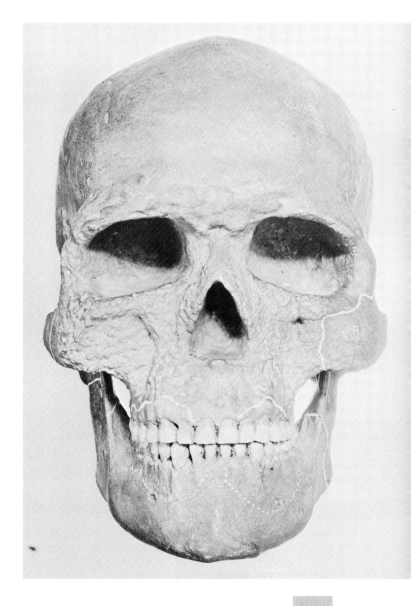

THE BEGINNING
OF HISTORY

As humans grew more skilled in hunting and more efficient in gathering plants, their numbers began to increase. Fire and improved weapons helped them to defend themselves against predators. For these reasons, the earth's human population increased quickly, and many groups faced the problem of overpopulation.

As time passed, the continuous gathering of plants made some vegetation scarce, and successful hunting depleted certain animal populations. People learned to cooperate, to make better tools, and to make efficient use of their resources. Despite these improvements, there was still not enough food to go around.

Any other animal species faced with a dwindling food supply and an expanding population eventually suffers mass starvation. This event drastically reduces large populations and ensures that survivors can find enough food to grow, prosper, and begin the cycle again. Such large death rates caused by overpopulation are common in nature.

Prehistoric humans, however, had developed tools and weapons, language, group cooperation, and the ability to contemplate the future and to solve problems. Using these skills, our ancestors learned how to grow their own food and how to raise large herds of animals for their meat and hides.

This change from food gathering to food producing resulted in a transformation in the human lifestyle. But the taming of plants and animals did not happen suddenly. Instead, people slowly learned which plants could be grown in large quantities and which animals could be raised successfully. Early farmers and herders also had to learn the best methods for growing crops and for taking care of their animals.

The Ancient Grain Belt

In late prehistoric times, the warm climate and fertile soil of the Middle East nurtured the growth of wild grains. About 15,000 years ago, the region's inhabitants began to use mortars and pestles (heavy bowls and small, club-shaped tools) for grinding the grains. While these people may not yet have learned how to plant the grains themselves, they had found a way to harvest this abundant natural resource as food.

At about the same time, the population of the ancient Middle East was rapidly increasing. As a result, demands for food were also rising. Toolmakers in the region crafted sickles—long, curved blades —to harvest more and more grain.

Humans in many parts of the world discovered how to harvest seeds and how to grow their own crops.

By 12,000 years ago, people in the Middle East had developed a way of life based on gathering, storing, grinding, and cooking grain.

Archaeologists have found evidence that by about 10,000 years ago, wild grain and some animal species were being transported to regions far from their original habitats. This change indicates that by 10,000 years ago, our ancestors had learned how to plant and harvest crops and how to carry the seeds to other areas for planting. Since then, farming has become one of humankind's dominant activities.

Agriculture was invented independently in at least two other regions. In eastern Asia, people learned how to cultivate rice, and in the Americas farmers grew corn. After humans learned how to raise their own food, they found many species of wild plants and animals that could be domesticated.

The First Settlements

When people stopped wandering and began to build villages, material wealth took on new importance. Settlers built granaries to store their harvested crops. Granaries allowed farmers to increase their crop production and to feed more animals.

Hunters and gatherers had valued land not for its soil but for the wild game and plants that the land could support. But when people settled in one place and learned how to grow their own foods, native plants and animals were not as important.

In places with good soil and sufficient rainfall, wild plants and animals were cleared away and replaced with domesticated plants and animals. For the first time, people began to own land and to consider it a form of wealth.

The Dawn of History

This new, agricultural way of life enabled more people to settle in permanent towns and villages. Since people no longer needed to move their shelters and belongings from place to place, town dwellers built larger and more elaborate houses.

Villagers began to make a wide variety of objects that would have been too heavy and bulky to carry while hunting and gathering. Heavy grinding equipment, containers for storing and cooking, furniture, and many other items became common.

As time passed, farmers claimed vast stretches of land, cutting down thick forests and driving wild game farther and farther from human settlements. The numbers of hunting and gathering peoples gradually declined as hunting grounds disappeared. Slowly, the agricul-

People eventually developed the skills and the tools necessary to raise great structures, such as the Parthenon in Athens, Greece. Built by the ancient Greeks in the fifth century B.C., the Parthenon has begun to crumble from the effects of air pollution.

tural lifestyle spread around the world.

Meanwhile, villages grew into towns and towns grew into cities. In the Middle East, the Mediterranean region, eastern Asia, and the Americas, great civilizations gradually arose in or near the regions where agriculture first began. With the appearance of cities and of written records, prehistory ended and the age of history began.

The Modern Era

In the twentieth century, most hunting-and-gathering societies have either died out or adopted an agricultural way of life. Several untouched groups, however, still live in the jungles of South America and on remote Pacific islands.

Many anthropologists predict that these cultures will also disappear as they adopt farming.

The human species has changed drastically during its millions of years on earth. As their bodies evolved and their brains grew, our ancestors developed the skills to make tools and weapons, to build cities, and to solve difficult problems. These abilities enabled humans to eventually dominate the earth.

Our presence on this planet, however, has caused a new set of problems. Pollution, overpopulation, and the loss of natural resources now threaten to destroy the earth's environment. But if, like our ancestors, we work together to solve these problems and to adapt to a changing world, the human species will continue to thrive alongside the many other parts of nature.

PRONUNCIATION GUIDE

archaic *sapiens*
(ahr-KAY-ik SAY-pee-ehnz)

Australopithecus
(aw-strayl-oh-PITH-uh-kuhs)

chromosome
(KROH-muh-zohm)

Cro-Magnon (kroh—MAG-nuhn)

fossil (FAHS-uhl)

Homo erectus
(hoh-moh ih-REHK-tuhs)

Homo habilis
(hoh-moh HAB-uh-luhs)

Homo sapiens
(hoh-moh SAY-pee-ehnz)

Neanderthal (nee-AN-der-thahl)

Olduvai (OLD-uh-vay)

Tanzania (tan-zuh-NEE-uh)

Taung (TAWNG)

GLOSSARY

archaeologist: a scientist who studies the material remains of past human life.

archaic *sapiens*: a subspecies of *Homo sapiens* that lived from about 130,000 to 35,000 years ago.

artifact: any object made by a human. Artifacts can include items crafted from natural materials, such as bone, stone, clay, or wood.

Australopithecus: the earliest humanlike animal. *Australopithecines* lived in Africa from more than four million years ago to less than one million years ago.

Archaeologists discovered this prehistoric chopping tool in Vietnam, a country in Southeast Asia.

This prehistoric cave painting in France reveals the skill of Cro-Magnon artists.

cell: the basic building unit of all living matter. A cell consists of a small center mass called a nucleus, which is surrounded by protoplasm, a clear, thick liquid. The protoplasm and nucleus are enclosed by a thin wall or membrane.

chromosome: a tiny, threadlike particle in the nucleus of a cell that carries genes, which pass on the inherited characteristics of animals or plants.

Cro-Magnon: the earliest member of the subspecies *Homo sapiens sapiens* to which modern humans belong. Cro-Magnons evolved about 35,000 years ago and lived in western Europe.

culture: the ideas, skills, arts, tools, and way of life of a certain group of people at a certain time.

excavate: to dig up and remove objects from an archaeological site.

flake: a sharp chip of stone used as a small tool.

gene: a part of a chromosome in which specific information for an inherited trait is stored. A gene transmits that trait from a parent to its offspring.

Homo erectus: a species of human being that lived from about 1.5 million years ago to 300,000 years ago. Members of *Homo erectus* were the first humans to migrate from Africa to Europe and to northern Asia.

Homo habilis: the earliest species of human being. Members of *Homo habilis* lived in Africa about two million years ago and made the first stone tools.

Homo sapiens: a species of human beings that has lived from about 200,000 years ago to the present. Modern humans belong to *Homo sapiens.*

mutation: a change in the chromosomes and genes of a cell. Mutations can alter hereditary traits.

paleoanthropologist: a scientist who studies the physical remains of prehistoric human life.

prehistory: the time before written history.

primate: an order (grouping of plants and animals according to natural characteristics) of mammals that includes people, monkeys, and apes.

species: a specific kind of living thing.

stratum: a separate layer of earth or sediment on an archaeological site that may contain ancient artifacts or human remains.

INDEX

A team of paleontologists excavates the fossilized remains of a dinosaur. The first dinosaurs appeared about 220 million years ago—215 million years before the earliest humanlike animals evolved.

A prehistoric artist carved this figurine of a woman (front and side views above) from ivory. The figure, which dates to about 34,000 years ago, is one of the earliest known artworks that portrays a human form.

Photo Acknowledgments

Visuals Unlimited/© National Museum of Kenya, p. 2; Independent Picture Service, pp. 7, 51, 53, 54, 59, 63; Australian Information Service/Photo by Percy Trezise, p. 8; Minnesota Historical Society, p. 9; Ed Gerken, Black Hills Institute of Geological Research, Inc. pp. 10 (top), 44 (top), 62; Virginia Museum of Natural History, Martinsville, Virginia, p. 10 (bottom); Annette E. Carmean and Jean M. F. Dubois, p. 11; University of Michigan Museum of Anthropology, p. 12; Office of the State Archaeologist, University of Iowa, p. 13; Bob Parvin, Austin, Texas, pp. 15, 49; Visuals Unlimited/© Cabisco, pp. 16, 33 (top), 41 (bottom); National Science Foundation, p. 17 (left); H. L James, Montana Bureau of Mines and Geology, p. 17 (right); Department of Library Services, American Museum of Natural History, pp. 19 (Neg. No. 2A8661), 34, 42 (Neg. No. 35919), 47 (Neg. No. 333193), 50, 55 (Neg. No. 109229); National Park Service, Alaska Regional Office, p. 20; Sam Valastro, Radiocarbon Laboratory, University of Texas at Austin, p. 21 (top and bottom); UPI/Bettmann, pp. 22, 46; Laboratory of David Ward, Yale University, from *Science* magazine, volume 247, January 5, 1990, p. 23; Geza Teleki/Hennepin County Libraries, p. 25; Library of Congress, p. 26; The Jane Goodall Institute, pp. 28, 29; The Mansell Collection, p. 31; Visuals Unlimited/© John D. Cunningham, pp. 33, (bottom), 41 (top); Russell Ciochon, University of Iowa, pp. 35, 60; Bill Munns and Russell Ciochon, pp. 36–37; U.S.D.A. Forest Service, p. 38; Stephen Mustoe, p. 39; Minneapolis Public Library and Information Center, p. 44 (bottom); American Lutheran Church, p. 45; Laura Westlund, p. 52; Tennessee State Museum, from a painting by Carlyle Urello, p. 57; French Government Tourist Office, p. 61.

Cover photographs: French Government Tourist Office (front) and Russell Ciochon, University of Iowa (back).